The Cogs *of* Life

Sabyasachi Das

Title: The Cogs of Life

ISBN: 978-93-5773-751-7 (Paperback)
ISBN: 978-93-5779-172-4 (eBook)

CONTENTS

Prologue

These poems are distilled thoughts and quiet certainties, shaped by the world as it moved around me. I hope these verses bring you a little light, as they have for me.

Origins and Reflections

Cuckoo! Said the Clock

Cuckoo! said the clock
Every day
On the dot.

The tree grew;
The child passed.
Cuckoo! said the clock.

The Watch's Watch

If your watch could speak,
What would it reveal?
Your character — would it revel,
Or betray what you conceal?

Circumstance

Circumstance decides
Where we go, what we win.
For while coal toils in a furnace,
A diamond shines on a ring.

Nature's Lessons

Lightning and the Wave

Do not love like lightning
Loud, brief, and bright
In the ink of night.

Love like the wave,
Wearing the hardest mountain
Into pebbles again.

The Stoic Oak

The solitary oak
Spoke to none.
No leaves, no flowers,
Yet its roots had run.

Through time, storms, and hail
Bark so thick,
It did not flail.

Then bird and bee drew near;
A tender leaf grew clear.
Spring arrived, and suddenly
The oak awoke in greenery.

The Earth and the Moon

The Earth danced
For eons alone
Mighty yet sad
In its orbiting zone.

Then a fiery rock came anew;
An earthly tide it drew.
Joyful Earth fell into trance
With the moon in endless dance.

The Lonely Comet

The lonely comet raced the galaxy
Resolute in its course, befriending solitude.
A boy looked up at the night,
Wishing one, two, three.

He smiled,
Took a knee:
For a comet streaked
Across eternity.

The Sea of Earth

The sea is salty,
Vast and deep;
It nourishes life
And guards our sleep.

It carried ships
And harbored dreams;
Vikings, merchants,
Empires' schemes.

It courted gods
And whispered lore;
Poseidon, Varuna,
And spirits of yore.

The sea is salty,
Eternal, sure.

The Forest Fire

A fire tore through the forest
Fed by greed, urged by lust;
Wind its ally,
Trees turned to dust.

Animals fled, plants aflame
Blackened stumps
Where life once came.

Pity moved a cloud's heart:
Rain fell,
Undoing fire's art.

The Volcano and the Sea

The sea was calm
Gentle, free
Embracing shores
With constancy.

A young volcano
Longed for an end;
Its fury rose,
Thinking the sea would bend.

A tsunami came:
A gift, a guise.
The volcano perished;
The sea kept its rise.

Love and Companionship

Love

There was once a star named the Sun,
In the void of space
Embracing warmth,
Darkness it did shun.

For centuries it shone,
Yet sadness crept in
As all looked away:
It had no kin.

Then one dawn,
A sunflower bloomed.
The sun's plight:
No more doomed.

For along came a friend
That admired only it
All day,
Till time's end.

Comfort and Support

The Firefly

The flower was sad: the sun had set;
Afraid of the dark, of the night it met.
"Don't worry," said the firefly,
Its ardent friend.
Carrying light,
The flower it would tend.

Tea

The tea tamed thirst

Timeless, true

Tempering tradition,

Tranquil too.

Be Not the Period

Love vibrantly,
Refuse an end.
Be not the period
That silences, friend.

Live your word;
Honor credence
Be not the period
That ends a sentence.

Rise

Rise,

Let not origin bind.

For a tree's trunk

Outgrows its root in time.

Power and Society

The King's Greed

The roaring lion
Terrified all.
Its jaws of greed:
Sought great and small.

Till a tiny snake
Struck, unseen,
Fate married death
To the jungle's king.

The Land of the Rich

The land of the rich
Reeks not of gold;
It glistens with freedom
And wisdom of old.

Where nightingales sing,
And ink outlives decree;
Where art is unbound,
And truth flows free.

Death of Democracy

Truth restrained, and freedom waned,
Silent presses, law unchained.
Ideas dim as questions fall
In marble halls where few rule all.

Power

The kings of old
Ruled with spears, spikes.
Today they bow
To shares, likes.

True power now
Rests in all palms
Zeros and ones,
Birth sacred psalms.

Prejudice

Prejudice kills,
Contaminates too
The brightest minds
It blackens through.

It turns a flourished heart
To a sealed tomb.
For prejudice kills
And spreads its gloom.

Power of Many

The power of many
Overcomes the one.
Ask the rat
That unraveled empires done.

The Book and Candle

The moon and star
Rule the night;
A book and candle
Set generations alight.

Wisdom

Knowledge seeks truth;
Wisdom fashions choice.
Like the old arrow
That ended many a voice.

Decay of Society

The largest bomb
Can end a day.
The death of debate
Rots society away.

Morality

At one man's crosshair
Lies another's end.
One man's terrorist
Is another's kin.

King's Crown

A king's crown
Rests not on the head
But on the blood
Of the fallen and dead.

Strength and Identity

Teamwork

"I rule the world!"
Boasted paint
Giving color,
Free of constraint.

"Not quite," said brush,
Without a blush
We give shape together;
Together, we hush.

Influence

Do not let proximity decide
Who can sway, who can divide.
Though the moon stirs the tide,
The Sun steers Earth's glide.

Strength

Do not confuse pitch for might.
True strength is quiet,
Yet steady,
And silently bright.

Light has no mass,
no measured size,
Yet stealthily illuminates
Worlds and skies.

Color

Color is a mystery.

A flower it beautifies;

A map it mystifies;

A bird it clarifies;

A flag it identifies;

But a man it divides.

The Lion and the Cricket

The lion roared;
The jungle shook
Its rule declared
Fear took hold.

Night soon fell;
A cricket sang
Soft and unseen,
A gentler clang.

Balance

The jaguar hunts
Poised, precise.
Predator, prey
The quiet splice.

Passionate, prudent,
Never boast
Death delivered,
Without a toast.

Diversity

Be together
But not alike
All trees are brown;
Yet no fruit shares a stripe.

Inner Worlds

Blind Faith

We pray to beings;
To books we bend
Warding devils,
Trusting pretend.

Faith can blind
Logic's heel
Fine-spun chains
On reason's wheel.

Hope

A man without hope
Is a gem gone dim.
Like a ship at sea
That can sink on a whim.

Disdain

To despise
Is to defame
Oneself concealed
In another's name.

The Honest Chameleon

Honesty flickers
Hard to tend;
A vibrant chameleon
Is all but nothing in the end.

Communication and Vulnerability

Stories Untold

To say it all:
Too traumatic.
To say nothing:
Too cryptic.

To say too little:
Mysterious.
To say to all:
Tedious.

The Brave Man's Relish

Fear and misstep:
A brave man's relish.
For even a diamond
Is never sold unpolished.

The Irony of Words

Words are a mystery
A language's tapestry.
Together, they tell stories;
Alone, they carry worry.

Written words are obeyed,
Rewritten, debated.
But the unwritten,
Remain respected.

The Black Hole

A star shared warmth
And love through light
To planets and comets,
Granting them sight.

Along came a black hole
With charming delight;
It befriended the star,
And bled its light.

Freedom and Horizons

The Cultivation of Freedom

Freedom thrives
Where the brave stand tall.
Even the finest painting
Falls without a wall.

Liberty

A movement for freedom
Begins with one, then three.
For every vast forest
Was once just a tree.

About the Author

Sabyasachi Das is a writer, traveller, and creative thinker whose work bridges technology, culture, and human imagination. He earned a Master of Science in Digital Marketing and CRM from IÉSEG School of Management, where his fascination with storytelling—shaped by both data and experience—took form.

Throughout his professional life, he has helped brands communicate with clarity while building meaningful relationships. His travels have broadened his worldview, and in The Cogs of Life he reflects on the quiet, inspiring moments hidden within everyday existence.

Written for a generation drawn to accessible, bite-sized insight, his poetry does not seek to decorate life, but to confront it honestly, briefly, and without looking away.

www.ingramcontent.com/pod-product-compliance
Lightning Source LLC
Chambersburg PA
CBHW062148160726
48282CB00027B/958
* 9 7 8 9 3 5 7 7 3 7 5 1 7 *